Leaning
Toward
the# Poet

Always a gap appears between a life event and its trailing expression. Lingering on one or the other side of the gap--gaping in wonder at what calls to be filled and fulfilled, Romanyshyn's book fills that gap with the beauty of its images that are at once haunted by the future even as they rest serene in past light. Written by a psychologist, *Leaning Toward the Poet* presents overtures to soul celebrating the ordinary.

Dennis Patrick Slattery, Ph.D. is the author of *Twisted Sky: Selected Poems* and *Feathered Ladder: Selected Poems of Dennis Patrick Slattery and Brian Landis.*

In his first book *Psychological Life: From Science to Metaphor* we as readers were invited to participate in "the recovery of psychological life as a metaphoric reality." Here in *Leaning Toward the Poet* Romanyshyn now extends that invitation again. This time, however, it is not through the application of any theory, or academic discourse; but, rather, through metaphor itself. In these pages one finds the poetic exploration of the wonder behind the ordinary, the phenomena of Provence mornings and evening light, as well as the "darkening plane (where) the dead are weeping" all brought to elegant life in this author's on-going response to, and recovery of, soul.

Brian Michael Tracy is the author of three books of poems: *Driving with Dante, Opaque Traveller,* and *The Distance Between Shores.*

Leaning Toward the Poet

Eavesdropping on the Poetry of Everyday Life

Robert Romanyshyn

iUniverse®

LEANING TOWARD THE POET
EAVESDROPPING ON THE POETRY OF EVERYDAY LIFE

iUniverse books may be ordered through booksellers or by contacting:

iUniverse
1663 Liberty Drive
Bloomington, IN 47403
www.iuniverse.com
1-800-Authors (1-800-288-4677)

Because of the dynamic nature of the Internet, any web addresses or links contained in this book may have changed since publication and may no longer be valid. The views expressed in this work are solely those of the author and do not necessarily reflect the views of the publisher, and the publisher hereby disclaims any responsibility for them.

Any people depicted in stock imagery provided by Thinkstock are models, and such images are being used for illustrative purposes only. Certain stock imagery © Thinkstock.

ISBN: 978-1-4917-4724-7 (sc)
ISBN: 978-1-4917-4723-0 (e)

Library of Congress Control Number: 2014955120

Printed in the United States of America.

iUniverse rev. date: 11/20/2014

ACKNOWLEDGEMENTS:

Front cover photo by Robert Romanyshyn

Thanks to David Rosen for his permission to quote
one of his poems from *Clouds and More Clouds*

Special thanks to my daughter Sarah Goodchild Robb
for her splendid drawings

Thanks as well to Lanara Rosen whose description of an attic
moment in a letter sent to me inspired "Dust and Dreams"

PERMISSIONS:

Sarah Goodchild Robb for permission to use her drawings

DEDICATION

To the poet in the dream---

the companion who guided me through the house of academia

to the threshold of daily life and its wonders.

CONTENTS

In the Company of the Poets

The Splendor of the Simple

Lingering in the Shadows

The Miracle in the Mundane

Stray Lines

A NOTE TO THE READER

We live in a time when we believe that everything can be explained. Psychology, whose roots initially lay in philosophy and since the late 19th century in the sciences, is not only part of but also is a major spokesperson for that belief system. Not surprisingly therefore most psychology programs now define psychology as a Stem discipline whose language is drawn from science, technology, engineering and mathematics. Humanities and the arts are being marginalized.

Leaning Toward the Poet: Eavesdropping on the Poetry of Everyday Life is an attempt to recover the neglected root of psychology inherent in its name: psychology--the logos of soul (ψυχή). My claim is that a poetic sensibility inclines us to the language of soul and awakens us to the mystery, ambiguity, subtlety, and the strange and awesome elusive epiphanies of the multi-leveled layers of psychological life as they display themselves in the world. For John Keats the world was the vale of soul making and in that vale the net of explanations loosens and our understanding of who we are is deepened.

The Introduction situates my claim within my life and work in psychology. Readers, of course, can choose to skip it, but it is the context out of which I write not as a poet but as a psychologist cultivating a poetic sensibility for the discipline of psychology.

INTRODUCTION

Almost ten years ago I had a dream in which I find myself in an ill lit and stuffy Victorian type parlor where a group of academics—philosophers and psychologists—many of whom seem familiar, are gathered in a circle in a discussion. Two details that stand out are how well suited and tied they are and how invisible I seem to be to them.

More than forty years ago I entered psychology through the door marked science and philosophy, and in the last twenty years or so I have been looking for the exit door of poetry. Between these two doors, psychology has been a good cover story for me. In the guise of the psychologist I have walked a bridge, turning at times toward the philosophers and scientists as companions at one end and then toward the poets as companions at the other end. But in those bridge walks it has been the moments when, with none of them at my side, I was suddenly stopped, which have had the most significant influence in shaping my life as a psychologist. A dream, an illness, the unexpected death of a loved one; the haunting sense of the past in the present; the first moments of falling in love or falling into a work; the surprise of the extraordinary that lingers in the ordinary, the spontaneous eruption of the splendor in the simple that becomes a moment of regard for what is so often passed by, and even the epiphany of the miraculous in the mundane: these moments always confronted me with the gap between the scientific and philosophic languages of psychology as a discipline and the logos of soul speaking from the abyss below the bridge. Leaning over the edges of the bridge to listen to these seductions would always undo the strategies of my map-making mind for disciplining soul. Eruptions from below disrupting the discipline of psychology! Always left behind in the wake of these disruptions has been the question of how might one re-imagine the discipline of a psychology that was responsive to the whispers of soul from below.

Being invisible in the dream to the circle of the well suited and tied academics, I begin to wander through the house and find myself in a room where a poet figure, whose guise and dress is vastly different than that of the academic colleagues, is speaking with a woman about the poet Rilke. The poet figure is dressed in shabby clothes, seemingly indifferent to how he might appear to others. His fingers and teeth are tobacco stained, giving the impression of one who, outside the margins of convention, has lived life fully.

The scene is erotic and I am jealous that the poet is with the woman because Rilke has been an important companion in my work as a psychologist. A mood of abandonment comes over me, and as I continue my wanderings I find myself with the poet beside me in a kitchen area where ordinary folk are preparing food and drink for the well suited and tied academics. They are talking with each other in loud friendly voices, and even at times breaking into song. The room is airy and light and filled with the nourishing aromas of the food being prepared and the fresh smells of early spring mornings. The poet takes me to a screen door that opens onto a sunlit park where many people are eating, playing ball and with animation and energy living and enjoying life. Standing beside me on the threshold, the poet opens the screen door and points in the direction of that scene. The dream ends there on the threshold.

In my more than forty years in psychology, I have been betwixt and between the philosopher and scientist on one side and the poet on the other, wishing that I could settle the tension between the two, but never crossing the threshold at either end of the bridge. Working on that dream, it has worked me over to the point where the image of the threshold now compliments the images of the bridge, the edge and the abyss as the places where I have been doing psychology. Although I initially called the dream 'Leaving the House of Academia,' the dream leaves me on the threshold between the worlds of the philosopher and scientist and the poet.

Bridges and thresholds! In their form bridges connect two different worlds. As such, bridges are places of passage and, in spite of those moments when I was drawn to the edges of the bridge to lean over and listen to the whispers of soul from the abyss below the bridge, bridges by design insist that one keep moving from one end to the other and at either end step across a threshold into one or the other world.

The dream's final image, however, implies there is something to be gained by lingering on the threshold where as a psychologist I am neither philosopher or scientist nor poet. While staying in the tension between these possibilities for psychology does not comport with my wish to exit the discipline of psychology through the door of poetry, the middle image in the dream, where a woman and a poet conversing about Rilke fills me with a feeling of jealously and a sense of abandonment, suggests that my wish has in effect neglected the connection between the poet and psyche symbolized by the figure of the feminine. In effect, in working me over the dream makes me wonder if my wish to exit psychology through the door of poetry has resulted in my giving only lip service, as it were, to the poetics of the psyche. Indeed, the shadow of that wish seems to be emphasized in the opening image of the dream. The well suited and tied academics, who personify a more philosophical and scientific approach to psychology, and who as such symbolize the way I have officially practiced the discipline of psychology, mirror how I no longer recognize myself in that way. Invisible to them I am no longer visible to myself as who I have been as a psychologist. And with this dream image the questions that have formed the wish to exit psychology through poetry have arisen again and address me as a challenge: 'Are the languages of academic psychology well suited to the sparkling speech of soul whose flashes glow in the abyss like fireflies in the night?' 'Are these elusive sparks dimmed when psychology, taking their measure, ties them up and ties them down either with its philosophical concepts and theories, or its scientific facts and explanations?' And in their wake and most important of all, 'who am I now as a psychologist?'

Looking back on his long life as a psychologist, Jung confessed that the death of the poet had to be the sacrifice required to create his psychology. *Leaning Toward the Poet: Eavesdropping on the Poetry of Everyday Life,* which has been born through this dream and its work upon me, is also a looking back. It is a step toward a memoir of my life in psychology, a backward glance through which I realize that as a psychologist, I have tended to cloak the poetics of soul in language that has remained wedded to psychology's academic styles of discourse. The irony here is that while it has been soul speaking through the language of dreams that has shaped my life and work in academic psychology, I have too often not only covered over and hidden the role of the dream in making that psychology, but also have tied down the dream in styles of discourse that are not well suited to the dream. And now it is a dream that suggests it would be unbecoming for me to continue being the psychologist I have become. It is a dream, which, in effect, says begin again.

Leaning Toward the Poet: Eavesdropping on the Poetry of Everyday Life is an experiment by a psychologist in animating the language of psychology by giving not just lip service but a full breath to the poetic life of soul. Guided by the dream figure of the poet who while lingering on the threshold points to the displays of ordinary life, this book is an attempt to bring more of that life across the threshold into psychology. It is an experiment in crafting a threshold psychology, which, in pivoting toward the poetic word, alludes to those fireflies in the night so elusive in their appearance and disappearance.

While untying the language of academic psychology which in its scientific or philosophic style seems unsuited to the more subtle appearances of psyche and ties it in knots, *Leaning Toward the Poet: Eavesdropping on the Poetry of Everyday Life* is not so much a leave taking of psychology as it is a recovery of it roots in the aesthetic, animate appeals of the world and a way of saying that is responsive to those copious displays of their mystery and beauty, a way of saying and knowing and being present to the *anima mundi* in its elemental epiphanies.

What, then, is this book? A psychology book? A book of poetry? I do not have any final definitive, once and for all time answer to these questions. I have only the questions, rooted in the love affair, ambivalent though it has been, with psychology, and this book as a reply.

If so inclined, one might read *Leaning Toward the Poet: Eavesdropping on the Poetry of Everyday Life* as a way of beginning psychology again. One might, for example, read it as an attempt to craft a radically different kind of introductory text for psychology, a text for a psychology of wonder whose language is rooted in a poetic sensibility. Read in this fashion, this book might be regarded as a book that celebrates, for example, the joy of seeing in words that are responsive to the erotic love affair between the animate flesh of the embodied eye and the seductive sensuous epiphanies of the world. I do not imagine, nor do I hope or wish that such an introductory text would replace standard introductory texts in psychology that explain seeing in terms of the anatomy and physiology of the eye. They do serve their role. I only imagine and hope that it would companion such standard texts, that alongside the language of explanation it would offer a language of wonder in response to those spontaneous epiphanies of the world before they are explained. *Leaning Toward The Poet: Eavesdropping on the Poetry of Everyday Life*--a psychology of wonder that unwraps the surprise of presence too long encrusted in layers of meaning!

But if so inclined, one might read *Leaning Toward the Poet: Eavesdropping on the Poetry of Everyday Life* as a book of sayings that are spontaneously responsive to what the phenomenological philosopher Merleau-Ponty in a pregnant poetic turn of phrase called the 'savage being' of the world. One might read it as a poetics of soul whose language is born in the natural alchemical rhythms of breathing, in that pause between the moment of inspiration when in-spired by the sheer 'thereness' of the world we take it in and then in the moment of expiration return it transformed to the world as a word. *Leaning Toward the Poet: Eavesdropping on the Poetry of Everyday Life* might be read simply as a book of spontaneous psychological ejaculations that rejoice in the splendor of the simple, revel in the extraordinary in the ordinary, sayings that follow the flesh of a finger pointing in surprise to the miracle in the mundane, sayings that open up clearings that bear witness to the stray lines, which, exposing us to the unexpected and shocking moments of the world, undo our map making minds, sayings as passing moments of dawn and dusk when the shadows of life and world show themselves in dark light, concealing themselves in their revelations.

But whichever way one is inclined, *Leaning Toward the Poet: Eavesdropping on the Poetry of Everyday Life* begins where the dream of nearly ten years ago ended: On the threshold between worlds. Perhaps that is the burden and the blessing of being a psychologist who is neither a philosopher or scientist nor a poet. Be that as it may, on the threshold I dream of a psychology that notices that there is a poem at the heart of everyday experiences.

A WORD ABOUT FORMAT

Some of the pages in the book have images or brief comments. The comments and images relate to the 'poems' that follow them. In addition, there are a number of blank pages that are invitations to engage the material in the immediacy of the moment.

Fireflies in the night,

a finger pointing

at a yellow moon

In the root of a word lingers the seed of an experience—

a com-panion is one who shares their bread with another.

*To be in the com-pany of the poets is to imagine a psychology
nourished by the bread of the poets!*

In the Company of the Poets

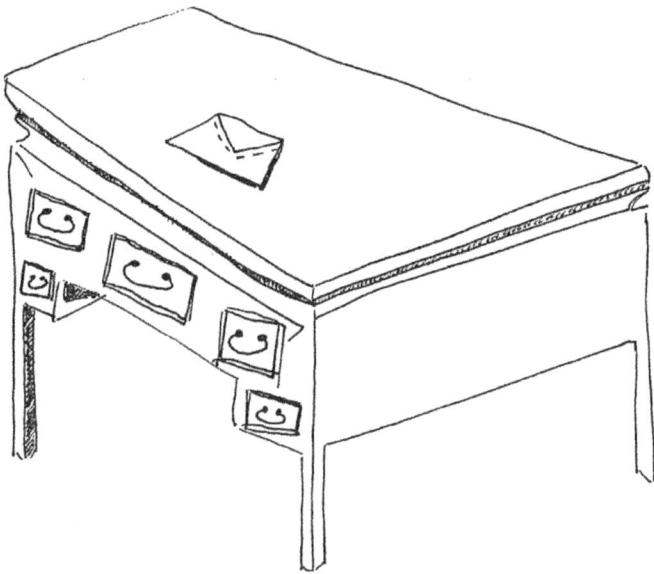

A POEM UNREAD

A poem unread,

     silent on an unturned page--

a letter unopened,

     lying on a desk

          of someone who has died.

Leaving academia…

        I join my friends

        birds, trees, and wind

                Clouds and More Clouds
                David Rosen

EXITING THE HOUSE OF ACADEMIA

I have been a standup comedian for the soul,
a juggler of passions,
a clown in a painted face,
a magician with a few bad tricks,
and a fool.

I have dropped milk-white semen words on many pages
and dripped blue honey in unsuspecting ears.
I have written articles and books,
traveled to far places,
made too many speeches,
ranted and raved,
begged and wept,
and made numerous appeals.

What is left behind of all these efforts,
of all these disguises?
Some legacy, some small trace of who I am, that I was here?
Are there any children of these deeds,
so many of which seem ill conceived?

On gray, empty days I see only abortions,
stillbirths and miscarriages.
And it seems I have wasted my seed and my life,
chasing phantoms.

I am getting old now and my days are long and slow.
I sit in the sun with a big hat to cover my face.
I have no magic to make the ghosts disappear,
and I am still a fool.

But at night in my dreams,
a poet sometimes comes
who leads me from the house of academia
into the streets of life.

When asked where his poems came from, W.S. Merwin claimed that he does not know and that the more they surprise him the better they are.

SWISS BANK ACCOUNT

Maybe it was a great poem,
or maybe only a good enough poem.
But it was a poem nonetheless.

It's gone now,
vanished because of his laziness.
It came in a dream, but he was too tired,
and anyway he did not want to disturb
the warm cocoon that sleep had fashioned around his bed,
put his feet on the cold floor, turn on the light
to search for paper and pen.
So, it slipped away, this at least good enough poem,
to that place where poems are kin to dreams,
leaving him only this feeble attempt to record its absence.

Someday, perhaps, it will come again in someone else's dream,
and they, less lazy, will write it down.
If they do, and it gets published,
is he entitled to claim co-authorship?
Can he ask for a percentage of the royalties?
Why not?
Did Frost write his poems, or the poems of someone else's dreams?
And what about Yeats, or Rilke, or Sappho, or Dickinson?
Maybe all poems should be declared the common property of the
dreaming soul.
And maybe all the royalties should be deposited in a secret Swiss bank account.
Then he could make a withdrawal on those occasions when he is not so lazy.

MR. ELIOT

I don't like T.S. Eliot.
I like his poems; it is the man I don't like,
or the image of the man I carry.

Poets tell true lies.
And they are useless.
We know that, or we should.
They are also fools.

But that is what makes them such good companions,
foolish souls to break bread with on the long and difficult journey,
bakers of bread too rough to swallow without some fight.

In the company of Blake and Coleridge, Keats and Byron,
of Sappho and Dickinson, Rilke and Rumi;
in the company of Baudelaire and Rimbaud, Ginsburg and Ferlinghetti,
of Philip Levine, Billy Collins, Mark Strand and Charles Bukowski,
Eliot seems far behind, at times even a false liar.

To be sure it is a clever thing to say we will know the beginning again
after the journey, know it like never before,
know it for the first time.
But from Mr. Eliot in his English tweeds and knotted tie,
with his thinning hair, like Prufrock, so neatly parted in the middle,
the words feel too neat, too polished, too wise.
Too controlled for me, too restrained.
I don't taste the blood in my mouth when I read them.
I don't die that tiny death that knows the hard price of the true lie.

I trust the fool, the thief, the drunk, the sinner, the depraved,
the hobo and the whore.
But, still, good company, even Mr. Eliot
close enough now to whisper:
"You are a fool, marching in a parade of fools
To a tune hardly anyone hears."

The Irish poet Patrick Kavanagh claimed,

with some sense of pride and more than a hint of gratitude,

that poetry made him a sort of outcast with his fellow countrymen.

MEETING PATRICK KAVANAGH IN DUBLIN

Along a walkway near the Liffey River in Dublin, Ireland
is a bench where the Irish poet Patrick Kavanagh use to sit.
I discovered one day that he still sits there,
even though he died many years ago.

'Trying to be a poet,' he told me, 'is a peculiar business.'
'What does it feel like,' I asked, 'to be a poet?'
But then a breeze rustled the leaves in the tree
and he was gone, leaving me with that question.

I have wondered about this business of being a poet for a long time.
I do not think of myself as a poet even though I do write some poems.
And I do read the poets, almost everyday, a kind of ritual practice.
But the word itself—poet—, it seems to me, is a benediction bestowed by others.
One does not bless oneself in this way.
Orpheus, I think, would be offended.

The tribe of the poets is a small one.
To join it, even if only to tag along at the very far end of their wanderings,
like some beggar picking up the crumbs of the feast left by those who are poets,
feels uncomfortable and even dangerous.
Prose feels more comfortable
and I feel more at home in the well fashioned costumes of my prosaic self.

But sometimes I dream
I am following along at the end of that procession,
wearing a patchwork garment
made by a rag picker from the odds and ends of life.
And the dream always ends on that bench beside the Liffey River in Dublin
as I watch Patrick Kavanagh sewing patches on the sleeves of torn coats.

ORPHEUS AND EURYDICE RE-MEMBERED

He, chewing up the ground in greedy steps--
                as Orpheus did in his ascent from the underworld--
the Dragons Hill yields to his pace.

She follows slowly behind him,
a hesitation marking her gait--
                as the grave clothes of Eurydice did so long ago.

Beside her, another,
weighted down by the slope of the hill--
                unlike the guide Hermes with his winged feet.

Higher up, the light,
so bright and sharp,
hurts their eyes.
Sheltering in a cove cupped in the earth,
they dream beyond time into the sky.

When they awake He and She continue alone.
The other one lingers,
spelled by the voices of timeless ones who whisper from below.

A cold wind winds its web around his form.
Between two worlds, he waits,
uncertain which path to follow.

At Duino Castle,

Rilke, knowing we exist

        in the gap between

Angel   and   Animal,

sang his elegies:

        Ten cries of lament and praise!

READING RILKE

A honey bee buzzing round a rose,

a brown bear stalking a frightened doe,

a breeching grey whale and a soaring bald eagle migrating home

occasion a vague remembering,

strange and hauntingly familiar.

QUESTIONS FOR PABLO NERUDA

On the floor of my study near the open window,
a fly, small, a black speck against the tan rug--
no broken wings,no crushed body--
lay quite still.

Was it sleeping?
I have never seen a fly sleep.
Had its heart just stopped beating?
Had it had a virus?
Did it die of cancer?
Do flies even get cancer?

Or, was it simply bored with its existence,
burdened in spirit by all the words in all the books in my library?
Was Heidegger's *Being and Time* just too much for it?
Or was it the dark pessimism about the human condition in Freud's
collected works?
But the poets were there, and plays and books of art
to refresh the spirit.

Small friend, if a window had been open in the music room,
would you have wandered in seduced by Beethoven's 'Ode to Joy',
and still be alive?

BEING WITH A POET

I saw Billy Collins in a pub the other day
Sailing Alone Around the Room,
while Lawrence Ferlinghetti was watching him
out of the corners of his *Coney Island of the Mind.*

I never knew this bar existed,
although others had whispered about it.
They said all kinds of strange things happened there.
Rumor has it that one day T.S. Eliot
actually spilled a Tom Collins on J. Alfred Prufrock,
while Emily Dickinson, listening to a frog,
shyly sipped some tea in a corner of the room near the fire.

I wish I could give you a map that shows you how to get there,
but no one really knows the way.

One day, maybe, you look sideways,
or you turn a corner when you intended to go straight down the street,
or you drop your plans for the day in the nearest trash can,
or you turn your cell phone off or even throw it away,
or you leave your identity on an empty bench in the park,
or you give all your money to the small boy with the blue balloon.

Any one of these things might do the trick.
But the real trick might be not caring if you will find your way back.

TAKING A WALK WITH A POET

I was taking a walk with Mark Strand along the same wooded trail,
the one near the hot springs of Sycamore Canyon in California,
where I first found him several years ago.

I was carrying him under my arm,
looking for that particular place on the trail where I had read his poem
"Old People on the Nursing Home Porch."

That poem, it seemed to me, was his version of the Odyssey,
but updated to fit the smaller, reduced journeys of ordinary folk,
of people like ourselves who travel highways marked with signs
that tell us where to go and how fast we may go to get there.

I thought of Cavafy advising us how to travel to Ithaca,
telling us to embrace the journey itself whatever it offers along the way.

I did not find Mark Strand today at that place,
but I did meet some companions,
some in a hurry to get where they were going,
others lingering along the way,
and even a few, enjoying the journey itself, stopping for an ice cream
on their way to the old folks home.

In the splendor of the simple,

    one might find

      the serenity of slowness

and,

    perhaps,

      even the solitude of the world's deep silence.

The Splendor
of the Simple

MORWENSTOW

An ancient Norman church,

stones lashed by winds a thousand years,

   endures

in Morwenstow Hamlet.

The dead,

  their chiseled names swallowed by time,

dwell beneath dark skies on moonless nights

in soil watered by endless rains.

WORDS AND THINGS

Do I write to ward off oblivion?
Are words shields against the dark pit of the grave?
Do I linger in green fields
when a sliver of sunlight offers redemption for a moment,
until drifting clouds shroud the sun
and I am in darkness again?

Words—I have traced my life with them,
have become their slave.

Writing seems a fool's game
whose cumulative effect too often is less than
one drop of rain drunk by a single leaf,
or the hum of a bee sucking a white Escallonia,
or a wood pigeon puffing its song
and flying away to the next valley,
to sing, like Keats' Nightingale, again and again,
indifferent to any trace or record of its voice.

Somewhere a green field spreads itself wide for the sun,
bees suck forever in the wombs of white Escallonias,
and wood pigeons unceasingly chant their songs.

UNTITLED I

Dawn—

barely beyond promise—

bird song,

mind,

       nothing divided.

BLACKBIRD

Above winter trees,

below empty clouds,

Blackbird-

these words!

BY THE SIDE OF THE ROAD

An old house,
      abandoned,
            broken down,
                  by the side of a road

wears its memories with a sad and quiet dignity.

UNTITLED II

I am still looking for
the flowers
dreaming under winter snows.

UNTITLED III

A child knows the sun does hide in the grass
where you can stub your toes on slivers of light
while walking barefoot through the world's green wonder.

SUMMER LIGHT

An old woman sits on a bench

with a few neighbors or friends

in the fading summer light

sometimes to gossip about this one or that one,

or sometimes only to pass the time,

or sometimes just to sit in silence and recall lost dreams.

EVENING LIGHT

Evening light is content with itself,
having already spent its noonday energies,
cleansed itself of its feverish wanderings,
rid itself of its manic compulsions to be of service and of use.

In the early evening,
light prepares to settle itself--
      again--
into the dark folds of the night.

MORNING RAIN

Wispy threads, nearly invisible amidst green leaves in the morning rain,

frame a spider's web:

A galaxy of silver stars!

A small, delicate miracle!

A holy prayer!

A temporary moment of natural grace!

SPRING MORNING

White curtain,

  a sail billowing in a morning breeze,

    the smell of an ancient sea.

PROVENCE

Quiet morning,

    Cool breeze,

        a European Goldfinch

            begins its song.

AN EMPTY BENCH

Under a tree
an empty bench
waits
for someone present now in his absence
who once sat there
quietly and alone.

DUST AND DREAMS

A dusty attic,

late afternoon light,

a child-- eyes wide shut--

dreaming with her mother's ancestors:

timeless in the many old photographs

piled in a cardboard box sitting between rafters.

SUNDAY MORNING

Early Sunday morning—

> a screened porch,

> two chairs,

> a small table,

> two cups for coffee—

waiting for an old friend.

ON GETTING A FOUNTAIN PEN FOR CHRISTMAS

It is time to write the world's masterpiece,

the one about the truth

    of being at home

    eating pancakes

    when the morning light is soft

    and it has stopped raining.

AT THE XEROX MACHINE

Standing at the Xerox machine, an ordinary day,
I noticed a red plastic ruler, the kind my father would buy,
along with pencil cases, copybooks, and new lunch boxes,
during the last day of his August vacations,
just before my sisters and I would return to school.

That forgotten world enters through that red plastic ruler:
My father's deep sadness, which he never spoke,
his sense of resignation at having lost the best part of himself somewhere,
long ago;
and my own sense as a young boy of his unspoken sorrow,
which over time settled in my bones.

Back then I thought that his heavy, silent grief was simply for the last days
of summer.
Back then I could not imagine that he was teaching me to mourn for lost worlds.

Now, ruler in hand, I am reminded of my own lost worlds and silent sorrows,
while standing beside a Xerox machine
on this extraordinary day.

Shadow work!

Epiphanies in Dark Light!

Lingering in
the Shadows

IN MEMORIAM: 1914-2014

On a blasted plane the dead are weeping.
They do not weep for us who,
deafened by the drums of war again,
stumble blindly into another dark night.

The dead weep for each other.
They weep for all who died
at Verdun, Passchendaele, the Somme,
for those at Gallipoli and Tannenberg,
for all who, on command, went over the top,
to be cut in half by the new weapons of war,
for all who gasped for breath in the trenches,
those slaughter houses of the soul,
for all those in that first world war,
the war that was to end all wars.

They weep with the sons and grandsons and great grandsons
who have followed them in the unholy sacrifice of blood.

In pale grey light
the generations of the dead are rising from their graves
throughout eastern Europe and the Balkans,
throughout the Middle East,
in Germany and France,
in Russia and England,
and the United States.

Shrouded in morning mist,
wrapped in their tattered and torn tunics,
their lament for each other fading,
they shuffle toward oblivion.

In the grave where they lie unremembered and unmourned
we keep killing the dead.

IN THE SHADOW OF CROAGH PATRICK

Ticking in a distant room,
a clock slices away moments of life.

A candle flame shudders,
frightened by the restless air moaning in the chimney like some hungry ghost.

A turf fire made some hours ago gives up its last feeble light.
No warmth spreads from it cold ashes.

Outside, the rough kiss of the icy wind off Clew Bay
turns the black fields as cold as a barren womb,
while Croagh Patrick broods silently over the tiny village.

The mountain, where the Devil's son was slain and snakes driven into the sea,
weighs heavily as God's law fixed in stone,
grinding the soul into the common soil that swallows all.

EDUCATION

In the classrooms of a university
you speak to the living dead.
Off the cratered walls of empty skulls
words echo,
while masked faces,
pasted with blank stares,
open mouths that drip cries,
like blood,
waiting for the next feeding.

CRAZY

Do you know this place,
newly furnished from Sears Roebuck,
freshly painted and decorated?

Do you know those who live there—
        the drug addicts,
                the sexually abused,
                        the depressed,
                                the suicidal,
                                        the legions of schizophrenics—
all those whom Frantz Fanon in a different context once called the
wretched of the earth?

Do you know this place administered as a place for healing,
where the cheery optimism of the staff with their pasted on smiles,
frozen orgasms from a time long ago, or never had,
walking softly on white rubber soled shoes,
go about the lie of repairing broken lives?

Do you know this place:
        a hotel for vagrant souls;
                a last refuge for orphans lost in the deserts of the human heart;
                        a sanctuary for the hopeless lying in the gutters of the
                        human mind;
                                a way station for the homeless drifting in the alleys of
                                a dark night?

This place:
A Greyhound Bus Station to nowhere for madmen and madwomen,
a warehouse for the damned saints
and holy sinners of the world.

NEIGHBORS: BROOKLYN, 1948

Pinch faced old women
in cotton house dresses
threadbare as their tired, old souls,
sit,
stoop bound,
in the fading summer light,
eyeing silent judgments
on all who pass by.

TWO PEOPLE

A man and a woman sit across from each other at a table.
She eats a piece of chocolate cake and drinks a cafe latte.
He too eats a piece of chocolate cake but drinks nothing.
They do not speak.
She, quite heavy, seems lonely.
Is she looking at him for some small sign of love?
He, quite thin, seems guilty.
Is he looking to her for some small sign of release?
When they finish only the scattered crumbs remain.

THE ORPHAN

Far from home, the stars in the black sky
no longer have their names, nor light the way.
Orphans limp along a long road with only hard bread and salt
and the bitter taste of life on the tongue.

Occasionally an orphan recognizes another orphan,
and they say to each other,
'Can you mend the wound in my heart?'
'Can you fill the emptiness in my soul?'

In the silence each knows there is no rescue.
There is only the road that seems to be going nowhere
to be trudged alone in worn shoes.

But sometimes when the sun has risen on the other side of the world,
orphans, sleeping by a dying fire,
stir with a dream of that moment when for a moment they were not alone.

MURRISK ABBEY: SEPTEMBER 15, 2001

On Clew Bay in the ruins of Murrisk Abbey,
laid waste centuries ago in the name of a god other than the one served there,
the wails of the dying monks can still be heard
in the wind that creeps around the broken walls and settles on the
un-flowered graves.

Was there one, or maybe two or even three,
who saw beyond the destruction and the chaos
a time when ruin would become monument,
and who, now in their ghostly dress wander unseen among tourists,
whispering their feeble, unheard pleas to not forget?

Steel, bent and twisted,
the bony ribs of two towers,
are frozen in a desperate leap toward the sky
away from its flesh of broken and fallen concrete,
of glass shattered and splintered.

A ruin made also in the name of a different god!

DARK LIGHT

We plaster over the cracks in the world
hoping the ghosts won't slip through
to disturb our restless sleep and haunt our midnight dreams.

We lie to the children, tell them fairy tales,
while in dark alleys young girls bend their knees,
mimicking a posture of prayer to a God who never really was.

The streets at night are soaked with blood
and the bum who lies face down in the gutter
chokes on the tears of the walking dead.

An old woman lies in a hospital bed remembering better times,
until Death grins at her door
and shreds her pleasant reveries.

DON QUIXOTE

Mementoes and souvenirs—
faithful sentinels waiting our return.

But the road is hard and long, the journey difficult.
Easy to get lost, to forget the way,
to neglect the fire that once burned so hot within,
to adapt, adjust, make concessions,
to compose oneself and forget one's foolishness.

In forgotten corners of life's attic
dust shrouds broken dreams,
while statues of figures that once inspired
lay in ruin in the fading twilight of a winter night.

READING CAMUS

Between the silence of the ordered, indifferent universe,
and our hope for meaning and purpose,
we dread the absurd,
rarely realizing the dread makes us human
and redeems the silence.

INTRODUCTION TO PHILOSOPHY

Don't ask for permission first,
            ask for forgiveness later,
                        but only if necessary.

Play dumb, act stupid, paste a vanilla ice cream cone smile on your face.
Say hello to everybody, grin like a clown, and keep your thoughts secret.
Don't tell, and then you won't get banished.
Say you don't know, if you have to,
but don't lie and don't cheat--
That would hurt your soul.
Just be as quiet as you can, go about your daily business like a ghost.
Stay hidden for as long as possible,

            and at night go home,
                        laugh, drink wine and make love
                                    with the one person with whom you
                                    can remove the mask.

WITNESS FOR THE DEFENSE

Stay long enough to be a witness for the defense.
Linger awhile with the bums and the whores.
Listen to the homeless and the crazies,
to all those without a voice.

The birds are still singing
but we are growing deaf and their songs are fading away.

The sky is streaked with blood,
but we are growing blind and see only white clouds.

The last days are upon us.
Note carefully the things that are passing.

Be joyful in the storm of frenzy.

GOD IS DEAD

By late afternoon almost everyone in the village
had heard of the events that happened early that morning.
A man, stumbling down the mountain,
had rushed into the village square shouting
"God is dead."

Those who had witnessed this strange occurrence
swore that he had a wild look about him,
and some even said he was the devil.

By noon the authorities had arrested him
and the local doctor declared he was insane.
At the trial the following day,
the doctor gave his evidence:

" God is dead?
Preposterous, unthinkable!
Are not our churches filled every Sunday with our pious, god-fearing neighbors?
Are not our merchants growing richer day by day?
Are not our enemies vanquished on the far away battlefields of war?
Are not our local streets safer than ever
since the village council passed the new security laws?

God is dead?

How absurd!
God is surely still in his heaven
And all is right with the world."

The wild man from the mountains was led away.

Left alone to his treatment in the asylum
he was soon forgotten by those in the village.
In time, with the drugs given to him to quiet his ravings,
he began to forget the strange occurrence of that morning.

Slowly he even began to resemble the people of the village.
His twisted braids of hair were shorn,
his matted beard was gone,
and his rags replaced by the uniform clothes of those in the village.
Later he even took his place in the community.
He married and, with his dutiful and obedient wife,
produced three children who were raised to be pious, god-fearing,
law abiding people.
A model citizen, he was made a member of the village council,
and toward the end of his life he became a deacon in the parish church.

After he died, his wife told her three children
how occasionally, when the mountain was washed in moonlight,
their father would rise from their bed and stare out the window at the mountain.
In those moments, he would tell her, he felt a strange fluttering in his heart,
and he imagined stripping off his clothes,
leaving his house and his wife and his children,
to climb the mountain.

Neither she nor the two sons could make sense of such strange behavior,
but the youngest child, the daughter,
now in the early years of her womanhood,
thought she understood,
because she too secretly felt in her heart the strange tug of the mountain.

Selena, for that was her name, disappeared one day,
no trace of her left behind.

Now and then some villagers whisper among themselves
about a wild woman on the mountain on moonlit nights singing her pagan songs.

To care for the world is to attend to its appeals to be witnessed,
        to be bewitched by its seduction of us to become part of its on going unfolding,
to respond to its desire to become conscious of itself through us.

To stop and pause for a moment,
        to regard the ordinary, to look at it again, for a second time,
might occasion a moment when the sheer 'thereness'
of the ordinary becomes extraordinary,
and, perhaps in moments, even when the miracle in the mundane appears.

The Miracle in
the Mundane

SITTING WITH V IN THE MORNING

It always starts the same way--
hot coffee, buttered toast,
and the newspaper, bought every morning,
set out on the table.

I like these few moments of silence before V joins me in the garden.
I like especially the cloudy mornings,
when the trees and flowers in the garden are still asleep,
their vibrant green still folded inside the darkness of the night,
and the birds are still at rest.
Now and then a hummingbird might hover over the Birds of Paradise
but its wings beat more slowly than usual,
as if it has not yet decided to be a hummingbird that day.
The mist that rises from the ocean effortlessly climbs the Summerland Hills,
carrying the water's dreams of green.

"I had a dream last night," she says.
The sun brightens, the mist begins to fade away,
the flowers and trees shake off their dark covers,
and the hummingbird beats its wings more frantically.

I wonder at this marvel,
of how the sun becomes more brilliant with the saying of the words,
of how the trees and flowers discard their night dress,
become more green and seem to stand at attention—curious?—
to hear the dream,
and of how the hummingbird now flits and darts among the flowers and trees,
whispering with excitement about what is to come.
But I also wonder if the ocean's misty dreams
are comfortable with their surrender to ours.

Now it is the two of us in the garden.
I turn my gaze away from the flowers, the trees, and the birds,
put the paper aside, take another sip of coffee and listen.
Making sense of the dream together, V and I are creating a world,
and I know that each morning we enact again the story of the fall from Paradise.

When she leaves,
when the coffee is finished or is now too cold to drink,
I look again at the flowers and trees,
I listen to the birds that are still there,
but now they are all a little farther away.

ON LOOKING AT A PHOTO

Was it raining that day—how long ago?—
when you left your house
and traveled to that place
where you sat—patient, poised and still—
as the shutter opened to let in the light,
slowly, so slowly, to fix your image?
For whom was it being made?
Was it for a husband, a child, perhaps a lover?
Your discreet Mona Lisa smile seals your secret.

In this old house
your image is fixed—again!—
nailed in its frame to a corner of a wall
by the stairwell.

Who are you? What was your name?
Did you live with joy, with sorrow?
Were you loved and did you love?
Did you wait for someone,
like Dido, abandoned in Hades,
did for her Aeneas?

On that day long ago was some compass set
for us to meet in the dusky corner by the stairwell
of this old house
where you now live—still!—
acknowledged, if unknown?

Your eyes the shutter that fixes me in place.

THE SMILE

Sometimes it happens unexpectedly
at the turn of a corner or at the opening of a door.
Joy radiates through the world with a smile.
What gods and goddesses created that radiance is unknown,
but only they could have created such a miracle.

Now, nearly forgotten, they sleep,
until someone smiles
at the turn of a corner or the opening of a door,
when they awaken,
and their laughter ripples through the universe as a wave.

ANIMA AND ANIMUS

I know I had some rough edges when I met you,
but I did not want to become too polished, a smooth marble.

I liked bars and the sweet taste of cheap gin,
the kind that rots your guts out if you drink too much,
while you, it seemed to me, liked elegance and beauty
and the mellow taste of a slightly chilled Pinot Grigio slowly sipped.
In the corner and on napkins I would write my wild thoughts
and you, silky and velvet, would laugh and round their sharp corners.

How did you do that?

Was the touch of your smooth hands the skin of my ideas?
Was your smile the soft flesh of my hard abstractions?
Was the curve of your breasts as you leaned into my words the acute angle
of my concepts?
Was the slope of your neck the fall of my thoughts into time?

A man and a woman sit in a bar and in that holy place,
sometimes the word becomes flesh.

FROM THE DARKNESS

Once, long ago--
late at night in the fog and rain on the streets of Berkeley--
waiting for a bus to take me home,
a fat man in motley cap and cloak waddled out of the mists
and whispered in my ear the secrets of ancient Egypt.

EAVESDROPPING ON TWO MEN SITTING ON A PARK BENCH IN SAN FRANCISCO

'No, tomorrow is a legal holiday.
The banks will be closed,
but the stores will be open.'

> 'So, maybe it is not a legal holiday,
> if the banks are closed, but the stores are open.
> Maybe it is one of those funny in-between days.'

'There will be no mail delivery.
The welfare office will be closed.
The stores will be open,
but the banks will be closed.'

THE WEB

Threads too slender for an unfocused eye,
the spider's web is invisible.
But fluttering wings betray
a monarch butterfly exhausting itself,
a fly its lonely companion,
and myself, also trapped,
in threads of sadness for this winged king,
and obligation to the dark lord of the underworld.

THE LIQUID YES

First,
Say, 'Yes, to Life!'
Only later, if ever, if at all,
Ask,
'Why?'

Let bird song and clouds, stars and moon
R
      A
           I
                N
like blue honey from the sky into your

Ear,

and stay still,
very still,
while they
D
      R
          I
                P   into your

Heart.

One day,
while dreaming with eyes wide shut,
magic might happen:

Flowers like tulips in spring,
might blossom from your mouth
on the wings of your

Breath.

Birds and stars,
clouds and moon
might scatter and become

Words.

Say, 'Yes to Life!
Be Glad!
Jump up and down!

Rejoice when a friend says,

'Look! V speaking Flowers.'

UNTITLED IV

I am moving slowly, as if in a dream,
my bones dissolving,
my flesh melting into the skin of the world.
A tree outside my window moves in the morning breeze—
a holy mystery!

I wear shoes and no longer feel the rough dirt on the soles of my feet.
At night I turn on the light and banish the stars.
Birds enter my garden in the morning,
but I am too deaf to applaud their songs.

When the sun begins its western journey,
I gird myself for the tuberous swellings
of the black green jungle outside my door,
and its tempting kiss of sweet oblivion.

MONT SAINTE-VICTOIRE

Two pine trees frame a green hill,
whose gentle slope is a woman's breast,
rising, as with a quiet breath,
to the gentle touch of soft white clouds.

A transient miracle already fading
as Cezanne whispers his desire
to paint one moment of the world's being.

NIGHT FLIGHT

Drifting in a metal tube
              30,000 feet above a patch-work quilt of earth,
the occasional cities below—
              islands of shimmering light in the dark night,
              radiant pearls strung on some invisible necklace
              fashioned by a madman—
have a terrible lonely beauty.

ROAD

The bend in the road beckons me--

    the curve of its turning,

        its twist away from my forward looking eyes

            a veiled promise of some great adventure--

A woman

    with a coy gesture or a whispered word,

        awakening an ancient sense of longing.

LUST AND HAPPINESS

Lust is no match for happiness.
Lust is a 40-yard dash, a sprint,
happiness a marathon.

For a short distance lust will do,
but for the long haul one needs happiness.

In a marathon one has to pace oneself
and run alongside others.
In a sprint one has to get ahead,
and leave others behind.

It occurs to me while I write these lines
that happiness is a large green fern
moving in the early morning breeze
and shining in the bright yellow sun,
when I can say to my lover:
'See that! Isn't it beautiful?',
while she says nothing but does smile.

Are these lines only for old men?

A few years ago a man who was 100 years old
ran in the New York Marathon.

THAT IS NOT MY NAME

She called, 'Robert,'
but he did not answer.
First grade, first day, first hour.
She called again,
and again he did not answer.

He was not deaf
nor was he day dreaming,
a complaint that would be made of him—
later.

She called a third time, 'Robert,'
and still there was no reply.

The other children,
their five and six year old bodies,
unused to being shackled,
squirmed in their seats,
eyes wandering over so many new faces,
wondering who was being called
on this first day in the first grade in the first hour.

She pointed her long, bone white finger at him,
and smiled slightly
as she beckoned him to her desk.

'Robert,' she said,
'Why do you not answer
when I call your name?
All the other children do.'

He felt neither shame nor guilt.
He knew why he did not answer.

"Robert is not my name,' he said.
'My name is Michael.'

In that moment
he knew that he would know
his name when it was called again,
even though that call
still lay many years in the future.

THE PUB: SEPTEMBER 15, 2001

Braided, blond haired Irish girl behind the bar

smiles.

Free of the weight of any visible sorrow,
her gestures seem as fluid as leaves stirred by a summer breeze.

A young boy, collecting finished meals from the tables,
inclines his head to whisper a question:
'Is the salt, Sir, sill needed?'

Four men, big in frame and strong in opinion,
drink their pints, talk, laugh, and drink again,
while a local family just come from Mass gathers around another
communion.

A ghost in this place, an invisible stranger,
I am a witness of transient acts,
mundane moments of grace that sustain the world.

Cold winds, creep through cracks in the old door,
whispering the terror and violence of a far off place,

Still, braided girl with blond hair,
wiping clean the stains on the wooden bar,
Smiles—

An ordinary miracle!

AN ORDINARY MIRACLE

As he does every morning,
an old man buys bread in the small village bakery of Fuveau,
and each day he begins his exchange with these words:

> 'Bonjour Mme! Comment allez-vous?'

In reply the baker woman says,

> 'Je suis très bien, et vous?'

And in reply he says,

> "Moi aussi.'

The old man then repeats his ritual prayer:

> 'Je parle français un petit peu.
> Puis-je avoir un pain grand compagne, s'il vous plaît?

The baker woman always smiles.
Does she appreciate the old man's efforts to speak her language?

Handing him his bread, she tells him the price.
The old man gives the baker a ten Euro note.

The baker slightly shakes her head to show she does not have change.
It is still too early in the morning.

The old man takes out all the coins in his pocket,
holds them in his hand,
and shows it to the baker woman.

She smiles again and takes out the money to pay for the bread.

The old man puts the remaining change in his pocket,
picks up his bread and says to the baker woman.

> 'Merci beaucoup, Mme. Bon journée. Avoir!'

The baker woman says to the old man,

> Bonne journée à vous M. Avoir.'

The old man exits the Boulangerie.

He is happy.

The October morning is cold,
the sky is very clear,
and the day is beautiful.

The Old man slowly crosses the square
and heads to Maison de La Press to buy his morning paper—
the International New York Times.

He enters the shop and greets the woman:

> 'Bonjour Mme!'

She replies in kind.

> 'Bonjour M!'

But today he cannot find his paper.
She notices his puzzlement and asks him what he is looking for.

He does not understand all the words
but he does hear the phrase, Que cherchez-vous?
and understands what she has asked.

He tells her.

She makes a slightly sad face
and says that today there is no International New York Times.
He does not understand the words but he gets her meaning.

She says,

>'*Désolé.*'

He says,

>'*Merci beaucoup. Avoir!*'

She says,

>'*Bon journée. Avoir!*'

He leaves the shop, turns right, walks up the street
and turns right again toward the *Boucherie/Chacuterie.*'

>'*Bonjour M!*'

>'*Bonjour M!*'

>'*Je vourdrais du jambon cuit, s'il vou plait. Six tranches.*'

The butcher slices the ham, wraps it in paper and tells him the price.

The old man can see the price on the scale and gives him the money.

The butcher gives the old man his change.

The old man leaves the *Boucherie/Chacuterie*
and crosses the square toward his car.

He knows that this is his last day in Fuveau.

He feels sad but also happy.

He turns the corner and is hit by a car.

The old man falls down.

A woman gets out of her car and bends down over the old man.

The old man does not see her.
He sees only an Angel.

The old man smiles, opens his eyes once more
and dies in Fuveau in France.

He continues to walk toward his car,
feeling how good it is to be alive on this cold autumn morning
in Fuveau in France.

Soul moves slowly and never in straight lines.

It meanders,

drifting off well worn roads

toward edges and margins,

pausing at thresholds,

inclined toward what has been left behind

and waits by the side of the road.

Soul loves to linger to witness

Stray Lines undoing our map-making minds.

Stray Lines

I AM NOT MYSELF TODAY

Some days as you are waking up, you might think to yourself,
'I am not myself today,'
and smile at the thought
before getting out of bed and starting your usual day.
But there are other days when instead of the thought
a soft voice from somewhere says,
'You are not yourself today,'
and that is an entirely different matter.
A voice that speaks to you like that is more insistent than a thought.
It is a moment of being addressed by an oracle, maybe even by a god,
and the self that you are is compelled to listen.

On those days you cannot go about your business as usual.
Even the first moment of getting out of bed is different.
Right handed, your usual and familiar self
puts his right foot on the ground first,
but when you are not yourself that day
how does the self that you might be leave the bed?
And then there is breakfast to consider.
Hot coffee, buttered toast with strawberry jam just won't do,
which makes your usual self wonder if such occasions,
when your usual appetites are unappealing,
are days when you did not hear the voice or just dismissed it.
But if you do listen, then the question,
'What does the self that I might be eat for breakfast'?
becomes a serious one.
Indeed, the self that you are even has to wonder,
'Does the self that I might be even eat breakfast'?

How do you go about trying to find the self that you might be?
Where do you begin to look?
A good clue might lie in the clothes closet.
Those shirts in the back that have hung for so long unused,
or the jeans that have been edged out by the fancy suits
might shout for your attention.

And the yellow sneakers that you—was it you?---bought on a whim
but have never worn seem to demand that you take them for a walk.
Tattered shirt, ripped jeans and yellow sneakers--
Is this the costume of the self that you might be?
And like Prufrock who wonders if he dares to eat a peach,
the self that you are wonders if some revolution has begun.

If on those days when a voice says to you,
'You are not yourself today,'
the self that you are joins the revolution,
then miracles might happen.
The self that you might be might do unexpected things.
He might, for example, take a long walk in the park and not go to work.
Or he might buy a kite and in his yellow sneakers
run with abandon in a wide field of purple flowers.
Or he might just sit on a bench and enjoy the delicious pleasure of doing nothing.
Or in tattered shirt, ripped jeans and yellow sneakers
he might even try to write a poem.

TICKET

The flashing red light awakened me from my reverie.

"You went through the Stop Sign," he said.

I could see the reflection of my face in his dark, cop glasses.

"Sorry," I answered, "I was day dreaming, writing a poem in my head."

"Poetry is a dangerous devotion," he replied. "The motorcycle is safer."

His pad was in his hand, his pen poised to do its task.

"Let me hear it."

"It's not finished."

"Say what you can."

I did.

He gave me the ticket anyway.

WORDS

Careful!

What if Words really meant what they said--

Forever?

Would I write this poem?
Would I risk myself in words?
Would anyone ever say to another, "I love you?"

Are words stones, marble monuments of dead visions and dreams?
Or are they closer to sunlight,
sparks of luminosity that illuminate things said and sung?
Or perhaps words are water,
fluid and flowing, baptizing this and that,
liquid moments.

WAITING AT THE DMV

Impatient, wondering if they will ever call my number,
and Kafka's nightmare now seems all too real.
The gray bureaucratic faces are as pale as the whitewashed walls,
their voices as hollow as the tinny sound announcing B-601 now being
served at window 7,
a number still too far from mine.

A very old man is sitting in a white plastic chair in a corner of the room,
and I wonder if he is dead,
or has just resigned himself to having become a number
sitting among the anonymous dead.

G-214 now being served at window 12, awakens me from my stupor.
How did the world get this way?
I do not remember a decisive moment,
a government decree imposing some momentous change.
It just seems that it happened slowly,
creeping up on us while we were too distracted to notice,
or maybe at night when we were sleeping.

I am trying to remember something,
how the world might once have been,
but my memories are as fragile as an old thread bare sweater
that can no longer keep out the chill of the coming night.

"C-615 now being served at window 10!"
I should tell someone that we should not forget lost worlds,
that what passes away should not be forgotten,
but my throat is dry and the words won't come,
and the old man in the white plastic chair is crying.

JUST THE TWO OF US

Then, you were the most studious one in school,
and we voted you the most likely to succeed.
Then, I was the class clown
who made everyone laugh.

Now, I trade stocks and bonds on Wall Street
and live in a swanky high rise apartment.
Now, you live in a cardboard box
And sell black shoelaces in Times Square.

The thing is, however, I wear only brown shoes.

A PASSING GLANCE WHILE DRIVING
A CAR IN A VILLAGE IN FRANCE

The boy slouching in the doorway
looks at the derrière of the girl with blond hair.

He smiles.

She looks at him looking at her and frowns.

He sees her looking at him who is looking at her
and is embarrassed.

She sees him looking at her looking at him
and is defiant.

The boy thinks of suicide.

The girl thinks of dancing.

In time the boy decides not to commit suicide.

In time the girl decides not to dance.

Later the boy goes to the university.

Later the girl goes to secretarial school.

In time the boy becomes a psychoanalyst.

In time the girl becomes his secretary.

He remembers looking at her.

She remembers looking at him looking at her.

They both decide it is their fate to marry.

They marry and in time they have two children.

The son, whose name is Pierre,

slouches in doorways

looking at the derrières of women with dark hair.

The daughter, whose name is Marie,

becomes a ballerina.

OLD MAN

I am sitting in a doctor's office feeling the pulse of my heartbeat.
An old man walks in.
He looks to be in pretty good shape,
tall, thin, with only a slight belly overhang,
like the kind you see on souls too long tugged by gravity.
I figure he is about sixty.
But his presence disturbs me, and I wonder if I look as old as he does.
Would someone coming into the office see two old men?
I fight the thought, turn away, leaf through a magazine pretending interest.
But he seems insistent, just standing there, searching in his wallet for his
insurance card.
"Medicare," he says to the receptionist.
He is at least sixty-five, maybe seventy,
and I feel even more disturbed than before.

HER

In the fading summer light of an English garden
your visible form was stitched to an invisible tribe,
your voice added to their almost inaudible chorus.
Along worn out paths crowded with those
who had neither eyes to see the pageantry
nor ears to hear the softer music of the spheres,
you traveled.
From that first epiphany
you have been harvesting the seeds of that moment.
So why fret now over those
who, long ago, could not see
the gleam in your eye?
The invisible ones are still waiting for you.
So, throw your arms wide into the air,
sing in a loud and wild voice,
and in exuberant ecstasy
be foolish and useless and you!

RED SUSPENDERS

Sitting on a bench
in a railroad station
where trains no longer stop,
an old black man in red suspenders
dreams of taking long slow journeys
on cool, grey-blue cloudy days
in the late autumn season of his years.

WHERE IS EINSTEIN NOW?

I want to live in the gap between worlds,
That place—do you know it?-
where things—and even people- might come and go,
unexpectedly, like electrons do in quantum jumps
that the laws of physics describe,
laws made by those whom we believe and trust-
scientists I mean-
who also come and go, appear and disappear.

So, where is Einstein now
as I sit in a café by the sea in Crete
watching travelers—are they all tourists?—
pass by and disappear?
Was that him just a moment ago,
or was it an old man with wispy white hair
and a bemused smile?
Am I dreaming I am sitting in a café by the sea in Crete,
watching phantoms pop in and out before my eyes,
which Descartes said convinced him he was asleep?

If I lose my mind,
leave it here on the seat beside me
in this café by the sea in Crete
could I walk away
and slip through the gap into another world?
Would I be dreaming?

GALILEO'S TELESCOPE

He pointed his telescope at the stars inviting the assembled schoolmen to look.
The moon, he said, had craters on it.
Too shocked by such blasphemy that corrupted its perfection,
they refused his invitation.
With their beliefs held firmly in place,
they retreated to their books and plotted their revenge
as their world crumbled into oblivion.

NOTHING TO SAY

I love the indifference of things,
how the green oak trees share their secrets with the assembly of elegant
flowers,
how the empty bench does not invite me to linger.

I have no place in this landscape so I hurry on,
ashamed of my desire to intrude,
and seek the comfort of my kind inside a room with a blazing fire
and the familiar chatter of their voices.

When they ask me to tell my story,
I whisper I have nothing to say
but silently think of the mute green trees
and the splendid indifference of things.

KEEPING IT SIMPLE

At the table the professors speak in solemn tones of ancient mysteries
after scrambled eggs and bacon--
having been cooked by someone else--
have been eaten and the strong, black, honeyed coffee has been drunk.

But the cook silently prays only to leave this place of too many words,
to sit in the garden under the white clouds of soft Antarctic ice
so still in the blue waters of the sky
until stirred by gentle breezes--
the sky's ocean!

THE COWBOY TRAIL

After a long hard cattle drive over dusty trails,
there is nothing like a good campfire and a plate of baked beans---
cooked by Gabby, who is older than God--
and uncorking a bottle of vintage Chardonnay
while sitting under starlight
singing songs from Broadway musicals
and discussing the latest Paris fashions.

ZERO – 1

This thing about names haunts me.
My own name shadows me wherever I go,
and I am not quick enough to give it the slip,
to lose it in a crowd of people,
or clever enough to slide it into the pocket of some stranger
and hide in stillness and silence in some dark alley
until he passes by.

Given to us by a stranger,
we are cursed with a name that chains us to a destiny.

Would I by any other name have lived the life I have lived?
Would I by any other name be the one who is writing these words?

Is the crime in the act naming,
or in the name that settles upon you like a shroud?

Have you tried to lose yourself in the vast open under the stars
even before the moon has risen?
Have you tried to leave your name on a park bench
next to an old man feeding pigeons?

In Loutro Bay on the southern shores of Crete,
where the winds of North Africa disturb the water,
Odysseus sways from side to side
but stays tethered to the shore.

AGING

Some days you wake up to the sound
of your joints creaking like an old door,
and you find it difficult to untangle
the cloth of memories
that has been woven round you by your dreams.
On those days you always know
soul pays the postage for sending you the dream,
but you, as always, pay the price.

How strange that the memories fashioned in the dreams of old men
are of youth and summer and beautiful women.
Stranger still is that the older one gets in time
the younger one becomes in one's dreams.

But the morning mirror is not deceived
by dreams or memories.
The mirror records only the slow,
sly victories of time's sharp knife,
even as the ghosts assemble—the friends who have died,
the children who have gone,
and most visibly the lovers who have betrayed
and been betrayed for so little.
A sad journey it seems; a folly,
this life, a serious mistake.

But there is coffee to brew in the kitchen,
hot, black and strong,
and eggs with ham to fry,
and toast, hot, buttered and jammed to eat.

So, as always, you wash the dreams from your face,
paste a smile on it,
and walk, a little more slowly and stiffly than yesterday,
into the day.

STRAY LINES

A boy beats a rug against a stonewall.

A dog barks nearby.

A woman in a brown dress,
bare shoulders slightly pink from the sun,
passes by.

Two old men order omelets and glasses of red wine.
They speak to each other in a language I do not understand.

A mother eats a sandwich.
Her young daughter eats pancakes.

The waves on the beach below break on the rocks.

A child's windmill—yellow, red, green—
Turns in the breeze.

A fly lands on a little girl's shoulder.
Her hand brushes it away.

A sweaty fat man steps into the street and is hit by a car.
His blood creeps into the cracks of the cobbled stones.
The man looks up at the sky.
A cloud drifts by.
His mouth is open.

The sky is blue except for the white cloud

Lightning Source UK Ltd.
Milton Keynes UK
UKHW041411010819
347167UK00017B/87/P

9 781491 747247